Saskatchewan
Scenic Secrets

Saskatchewan
Scenic Secrets

Robin and Arlene Karpan

PARKLAND PUBLISHING

Saskatoon

Published in Canada in 2001 by

Parkland Publishing
501 Mount Allison Place
Saskatoon, Saskatchewan
Canada S7H 4A9

Telephone: (306) 242-7731
e-mail: info@parklandpublishing.com
web site: www.parklandpublishing.com

Second printing 2003
Third printing 2008

Printed in Canada by Friesens.

Canadian Cataloguing in Publication Data

Karpan, Robin.
    Saskatchewan scenic secrets
    ISBN 10: 0-9683579-3-8
    ISBN 13: 978-09683579-3-4

1. Saskatchewan--Pictorial works. 2. Wilderness areas--Saskatchewan--Pictorial works. I. Karpan, Arlene. II. Title.

FC3512.K37 2001   971.24'03'0222   C2001-910111-2
F1071.8.K37 2001

TITLE PAGE: *Sandstone cliff in Souris River valley.*
SECOND PAGE: *Castle Butte at sunset, Big Muddy Badlands.*
OPPOSITE: *Northern lights on the Churchill River.*
FOLLOWING: *Fall in the Spruce River valley, Prince Albert National Park.*

Acknowledgements

We thank the many people who assisted us in our research by fact checking and offering useful comments and suggestions on the text and photographs.

Parkland Publishing gratefully acknowledges the financial assistance of the Cultural Industries Development Fund in the production of this book, as well as the assistance provided by the following sponsors: Tourism Saskatchewan, Nature Saskatchewan, Saskatchewan Outdoor and Environmental Education Association.

Contents

Introduction

Saskatchewan Scenic Secrets is a visual journey across Saskatchewan, from the deep south to the far north, through all of the province's diverse ecoregions, to where the beauty of nature takes centre stage. Saskatchewan's special places are everywhere, from popular parks to little-known and little-visited gems that truly are "secrets". While some are hidden in remote wilderness, a surprising number are practically in our back yards, accessible to anyone with the motivation to venture off the beaten path.

Saskatchewan is best known as a "prairie province", perhaps not surprising when we consider the history of settlement. While prairie is certainly a defining characteristic, it is only one part of the fascinating story of Saskatchewan's natural landscapes.

Saskatchewan is rolling grasslands disappearing into a distant horizon, with not a tree in sight, but it is also thick forest with 20-metre tall trees. Saskatchewan is arid badlands with eroded buttes and silvery sage, but it is also lush green valleys and secluded sanctuaries where carpets of ferns thrive under a forest canopy. The Saskatchewan landscape is rife with superlatives: some of the largest tracts of uncultivated grasslands left on the Great Plains, the largest sand dunes in Canada, wetlands of international significance, and wild pristine rivers rushing through deep canyons and over magnificent waterfalls. No one landscape typifies Saskatchewan. Indeed, the Saskatchewan landscape is best defined by its incredible diversity.

Looking at the big picture, Saskatchewan has four major Ecozones – broad divisions of major physical features, further divided into eleven Ecoregions (see map on page 124). Just over a third of the province lies within the Prairie Ecozone, including the vast grasslands of the southwest, most of Saskatchewan's agricultural land, and aspen parkland where aspen groves mix with fescue grasslands. An oddity in the Prairie Ecozone is the Cypress Hills Uplands where elements of forest and alpine landscapes meld with prairie.

Moving north, the Boreal Plain Ecozone is a wide band across the middle of Saskatchewan, covering just over a quarter of its land mass. Here we find the northern reaches of agriculture and the beginning of the great boreal forest, dominated by coniferous trees such as pine, spruce and tamarack.

Further north, we enter the Boreal Shield Ecozone, covering close to a third of the province. As the name suggests, boreal forest is associated with the Canadian Shield, characterized in many places by massive outcroppings of Precambrian rock, some of the oldest on earth.

The most northerly and smallest Ecozone is the Taiga Shield. Sometimes called the "Land of Little Sticks", this is a transition area where stunted widely-spaced trees are scattered amongst innumerable bogs and wetlands as we approach the tundra further north.

Saskatchewan Scenic Secrets is a celebration of the beauty of nature, but we also hope that the book will help to raise awareness of Saskatchewan's special natural places and the need to conserve them. The story of Saskatchewan landscapes is both good news and bad news – the good news is that we have such a rich variety of beautiful

Elm trees and ostrich ferns along the Red Deer River in northeastern Saskatchewan.

natural areas; the bad news is that many are endangered spaces that are disappearing at an alarming rate.

We cannot imagine a Saskatchewan without natural prairie, where lavender crocus blossoms announce the arrival of spring, and sage grouse perform their age-old mating rituals. Nor can we imagine a Saskatchewan without canoe trips down clear northern rivers running wild and free, where no signs of "civilization" intrude on a wilderness experience lost to most of the world. When deciding how land is used, we hope that some day governments will not only look at what land does for the economy, but also at what the beauty of nature does for our souls.

Cypress Hills

The Cypress Hills' eyecatching displays of wild-flowers and orchids are due in large part to the variety of habitats. The sticky geranium shown here blooms in June and July.

The landscape of the Cypress Hills is like no other in Saskatchewan. With sweeping vistas and a mosaic of forest and grasslands, the hills rise 600 metres above the surrounding plain – the highest elevation in mainland Canada between the Rockies and Labrador. While the Cypress Hills lie within the Prairie Ecozone, they also have a lot in common with northern forest and alpine areas.

During the last Ice Age, glaciers flowed around the hills but never completely covered them. The surrounding land was further sculpted by the ice sheets and reworked by meltwater as the glaciers retreated. The tops of these hills, along with parts of the Wood Mountain Upland to the east, were the only parts of Saskatchewan not covered by glaciers.

OPPOSITE: *Battle Creek Valley in the West Block of Cypress Hills Interprovincial Park.*

Along with the vegetation of mixed grass prairie and rough fescue grasslands are species that are more representative of alpine areas or the foothills of the Rockies such as purple clematis, heart-leaved arnica and yellow monkeyflower. This is the only place in Saskatchewan to have lodgepole pines, whose tall straight trunks were used for tipi poles.

Some wildlife found in the hills, such as elk and moose, are more typical of the northern forest. Among the more than 240 bird species are some that are rarely found in other areas of Saskatchewan, such as dusky flycatchers and MacGillivray's warblers. Trumpeter swans, hunted almost to the point of extinction in the 1930s, have nested at Adams Lake.

Cypress Hills Interprovincial Park encompasses two blocks in Saskatchewan and another in Alberta. The two Saskatchewan blocks are separated by the Gap, a rolling tract of grazing land that is typical knob and

kettle country. Higher knobs originated from glacial till, while kettles originated from embedded blocks of glacial ice that left deep depressions in the soil when they melted.

Strangely, the one thing you won't find in the Cypress Hills is cypress trees. Early French Canadian explorers named this area *Montagne de Cypres*, mistaking the lodgepole pine for eastern jack pine which they knew as *cypres*, or cypress.

OPPOSITE TOP LEFT: *Bald Butte, the highest point in the Centre Block of Cypress Hills Interprovincial Park, looks over the plains below.*
OPPOSITE BOTTOM LEFT: *Red three-flowered avens blanket the grasslands of the Gap.*
OPPOSITE RIGHT: *The "hidden" conglomerate cliffs overlook Battle Creek Valley. They are called "hidden" because they can not be seen from the valley below. These cliffs are only accessible by hiking along the Trans Canada Trail.*
ABOVE: *The first rays of morning sunshine light up the Conglomerate Cliffs, formations of small rounded stones that have been naturally cemented together by calcium carbonate that emerged from groundwater.*

ABOVE: *Battle Creek, flowing through the West Block of Cypress Hills Interprovincial Park, is the northern extent of the Mississippi watershed.*

OPPOSITE: *The view over Adam's Lake shows the diversity of the Cypress Hills. South-facing hills are sunny and windswept while mixed forest covers moister north-facing slopes.*

OPPOSITE AND ABOVE: *Near Eastend, named for its location at the east end of the Cypress Hills, eroded slopes along the Frenchman River Valley expose layers dating back as far as 65–75 million years ago when dinosaurs roamed the earth. It was near here that "Scotty" was discovered, the first Tyrannosaurus* rex *skeleton found in Saskatchewan and one of few in the world. A striking feature of the hills is the wide band of whitemud near the base, consisting primarily of kaolinized sandstone. Kaolin is soft white clay that is highly regarded in the ceramics industry because of its ability to remain bright white even after firing.*

The Frenchman River Valley in Grasslands National Park.

Grasslands

While most of the prairie has been converted to agriculture, areas of native grasslands can still be found throughout southern Saskatchewan.

The countryside in and around Grasslands National Park in the southwest is one of the largest tracts of undisturbed mixed grass prairie in North America. The vast landscape encompasses deeply incised coulees, high weathered buttes, and the wide Frenchman River Valley, formed 10,000 years ago as a glacial meltwater channel.

This was the land of the bison and the ancient hunting grounds of Assiniboine, Gros Ventre, Blackfoot and Cree who returned here year after year because it provided the only reliable water for miles around. Later it became the land of the cowboy and sprawling cattle ranches. Today most of the land is still used for grazing, although Parks Canada is gradually acquiring land for the national park.

Perhaps here, more than anywhere in Saskatchewan, you can feel the boundless space, where an endless sky meets a sea of grass, and you truly believe that you can see forever. Among the special places is 70-Mile Butte just south of Val Marie. Rising 100 metres above the valley floor, the promontory was named by early North West Mounted Police because it was 70 miles from Wood Mountain on their patrol trail to Fort Walsh in the Cypress Hills.

Part of the Mixed Grassland Ecoregion, the main vegetation, as expected, is grass – primarily spear grass, wheatgrass and blue grama grass. Variety and color are added by sage, a profusion of wildflowers such as crocus, cinquefoil, aster and fleabane, and a surprising amount of lichen.

Climb the hillsides and tall buttes and you might swear that there isn't a tree growing anywhere in the country. But down on the valley floor, especially near the river, stands of buffaloberry, wolf willow, and pockets of

Black-tailed prairie dog.

green ash and aspen provide a haven for songbirds and cover for deer.

Wildlife is an integral part of these grasslands. Pronghorn antelope, white-tailed deer, mule deer and coyotes are common. You might hear the piercing screams of golden eagles or rare ferruginous hawks. Several threatened or endangered species call this valley home – sage thrasher, burrowing owl, loggerhead shrike, and mountain plover to mention a few. This is one of the few places in Saskatchewan, and indeed Canada, to see prairie rattlesnakes, as well as the only place in Canada where black-tailed prairie dogs live. The Frenchman River Valley is among the last refuges for endangered sage grouse, which in Canada survive only in a small part of southwest Saskatchewan and southeast Alberta.

ABOVE: *Pronghorn antelope.*
LEFT: *Male sage grouse try to impress a female with an elaborate courtship display.*
OPPOSITE: *Hills and buttes south of Val Marie.*

ABOVE: *The character of the grasslands changes with the changing light. Here, storm clouds parted for a few moments just before sunset.*

OPPOSITE: *Grasslands in the Old Man On His Back area of southwest Saskatchewan.*

Badlands

OPPOSITE AND ABOVE: *Killdeer Badlands.*

S olitary buttes with weather-beaten faces stand in defiance of centuries of erosion. Stone-capped hoodoos shelter pillars of fragile earth in stark valleys that seem from another world. Sage and cactus seek out moist cracks in sun-baked soil stingy with its life-giving sustenance. Such are Saskatchewan's badlands, "bad" perhaps in their grudging toleration of life, yet striking in their austere beauty.

Killdeer Badlands

Badlands dot the Saskatchewan landscape, primarily in the hot, semi-arid grasslands of the deep south. The Killdeer Badlands south of Wood Mountain are the "baddest" of them all – big, rough and untamed. Just north of the Montana border, the rolling grassland plateau suddenly drops into a deep valley with sharply gullied slopes and free-standing buttes. Some buttes have flat tops, remnants of the plateau that has disappeared around them. Others are embellished with red or white cone-like tops, while a few are so whimsically shaped that they could pass for abstract art.

The eroded slopes reveal a geological story going back millions of years to when dinosaurs reigned. Indeed, it was in these fossil rich badlands that George Mercer Dawson, a geologist working with the Boundary Commission, discovered the first dinosaur bones in western Canada in 1874.

Sparse as it may seem, life continues in this arid land. Cattle graze on native grasses on the plateau, then make the downhill trek to the valley bottom to water in tiny creeks that were once minor spillways created by glacial meltwater.

While most of the land in this area remains privately run pasture, some is part of the East Block of Grasslands National Park. Parks Canada is gradually expanding its holdings here as land comes up for sale.

Erosion has caused deeply-etched patterns on buttes and hillsides in the Big Muddy Valley.

Big Muddy Badlands

South of Bengough, the prairie opens up into the Big Muddy Badlands. And muddy it is. Sides of buttes and hills look as if they are dripping like an icing-covered chocolate cake left too long in the sun. If you come here after a rain, it will feel like melted chocolate as well, only stickier.

The Big Muddy is part of a wide valley formed by glacial meltwater over 15,000 years ago. Continuing erosion has molded the slopes, rounded the hilltops and cut deeper channels revealing layers of multi-colored sediment deposited over millions of years. Valley slopes are important habitat for nesting prairie falcons, golden eagles and several species of hawks. Most of the rolling grasslands are used for grazing.

This wild land has a long history, back to when early people of the Great Plains arranged stone effigies to represent a turtle, a buffalo, and patterns whose significance have been lost in time. Later it became the domain of the cowboy, of sprawling ranches and Mounted Police on horse patrols trying to keep law and order.

For Big Muddy outlaws, the high hills and buttes were ideal lookouts, while wooded coulees made handy hideouts. Notorious cattle and horse thieves the likes of Dutch Henry went a step further and hid out in

Layers of sediment dating back millions of years are revealed in eroded slopes in the Big Muddy Badlands.

isolated hillside caves. For Butch Cassidy and the Wild Bunch, Big Muddy was Station No. 1 on the famed Outlaw Trail that ran south all the way to Mexico.

Castle Butte towers above the valley floor. This 60-metre high monolith was an important landmark for Plains Indians, early settlers, Mounted Police patrols and outlaws.

Castle Butte imparts both the power and fragility of nature. Up close, its deeply incised walls appear to be melting away, while the steep path to the top is crumbling from years of wear. Yet when we move back and look at the whole, the castle-like majesty is unmistakable. Castle Butte at sunrise ranks among southern Saskatchewan's most magnificent sights. When the sun clears the eastern horizon, it immediately floods the flat-topped butte with a brilliant crimson glow that is both powerful and mystical.

OPPOSITE: *At dawn, the first rays of sunlight illuminate Castle Butte.*
ABOVE: *Castle Butte has long been a prominent landmark in the Big Muddy Valley.*

OPPOSITE AND RIGHT: *Near the town of Avonlea, and next to Avonlea Creek, the gently undulating grassland is broken by a pocket of beautiful badland gullies. Located entirely on private pasture, the badlands give no hint of their whereabouts until you reach the valley rim and the view below unfolds.*

ABOVE: *A small hoodoo stands in a badland valley in a community pasture near Halbrite.*

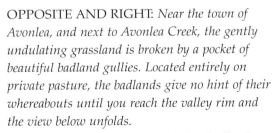

Southern Dunes

Sand dunes in Douglas Provincial Park near Lake Diefenbaker.

Sand dunes are intriguing, desert-like islands in a sea of grassland, farmland, parkland and boreal forest. So significant are Saskatchewan dunes that noted geologist and dune expert, Peter David, wrote that "Saskatchewan dune occurrences hold the greatest variety of dune forms and dune associations in the whole of Canada."

Great Sand Hills

Covering close to 2,000 square kilometres of southwest Saskatchewan between the Trans Canada Highway and the South Saskatchewan River, the Great Sand Hills are the largest continuous sand dunes in southern Canada. The only larger expanse of dunes is the Athabasca Sand Dunes in northern Saskatchewan.

OPPOSITE: *Ripples on the face of an active dune in the Great Sand Hills.*

Sand deposited here by the retreat of the glaciers has been reworked by the wind over the years. Today these semi-arid hills, located in the Mixed Grassland Ecoregion, are a combination of stabilized sand hills, active dunes, and prairie grasses interspersed with low bushes and shrubs. The ubiquitous sage gives much of the land a silvery appearance and a distinctive fragrance.

Although active dunes account for only .5% of the area, they are clearly the most striking feature of the sand hills. South of Sceptre, the terrain becomes more sandy and grain fields give way to rolling grazing land. Then suddenly you see them – massive walls of sand, covered with wind-sculpted ripples, rising from the level prairie as high as a two-story building.

The vast unploughed prairie in the Great Sand Hills supports a wide array of prairie wildlife including pronghorn antelope, coyote and sharp-tailed grouse. It is critical habitat for one of the largest mule deer populations in Saskatchewan, and home to rare Ord's kangaroo rats. These tiny rodents are able to convert dry seeds into water, an important adaptation for surviving in an arid climate.

Douglas Dunes

Sand dunes near the east shore of Lake Diefenbaker are protected in Douglas Provincial Park. They were formed when rivers and streams carrying glacial meltwater deposited sand and other sediment in a delta. When the waterways dried, large areas were exposed to the ravages of the wind, which continues to rework the sand.

The Douglas Dunes are among the most accessible sand dunes in Saskatchewan, reached by a hiking trail from the aptly named Dunes Nature Centre. When you're in the midst of these dunes, you feel like you have been transported somewhere remote and exotic. The effects of the relentless wind are obvious in deeply scoured blowouts and depressions, and in the exposed roots of trees and shrubs that have been undermined as the supporting sand is blown away. Blades of grass have been whipped around, leaving perfect circles in the sand, as if drawn by a compass.

Good Spirit Dunes

The dunes of Good Spirit Lake in eastern Saskatchewan are different again. Located

OPPOSITE: *Vegetation has a tough time surviving in the active sand dunes in Douglas Provincial Park.*
RIGHT: *Dunes on the shore of Good Spirit Lake.*

in aspen parkland, the countryside around Good Spirit Lake tends to be green, lush and well treed, not at all desert-like.

The dunes originated in glacial times when an ancient river dried, leaving behind sandy sediment. Strong prevailing northwesterly winds carried exposed sand to the southeast, depositing it in ridges that eventually grew into dunes. Years later, when wetter conditions returned, water collected in the sandy basin which became Good Spirit Lake. The northern end is the deepest, where a large blowhole was formed when sand was carried away, while the water next to the dunes is extremely shallow.

The dunes stretch for about five kilometres in a wide band along the south and east shores of the lake. Short vegetation grows along the fine sandy beach with thicker stands of shrubs and trees farther back where moisture is caught between the ridges.

When Good Spirit experiences a year or two of low water, the look of the beach and dunes can change very quickly. More sand exposed along the shallow south and east shores is driven into ridges by the waves. Tiny plants start to appear in the moist sand along the wide beach, eking out a tenuous existence in nutrient deficient conditions. All this can change yet again when high water returns, flooding the tiny plants and ripping apart the new beach ridge.

When the lake level is low, numerous sand bars form along the beach of Good Spirit Lake.

Prairie River Valleys

South Saskatchewan River

The South Saskatchewan is the big daddy of prairie rivers. Grand and powerful, it cuts through southern and central Saskatchewan, changing its face as it flows from the Alberta border to the Saskatchewan River Forks where it joins the North Saskatchewan. Most noticeable are the valley slopes which gradually change from treeless grasslands to mixed wood forest.

A spectacular stretch is near the Red Deer Forks just east of the Alberta border where the Red Deer River joins the South Saskatchewan. High rolling hills drop steeply to the valley floor, their eroded slopes in places resembling badland formations. The wide deep valleys of both rivers converge at the forks forming a six-kilometre wide double valley, the likes of which occurs nowhere else in Saskatchewan.

The rugged terrain is primarily short grass prairie fenced for private pasture. Treeless hills give way to wooded river flats near the forks where one of Saskatchewan's largest stands of cottonwoods is found.

In rainy summers, the normally arid grasslands come alive with color – showy bright pink wild roses in low spots, and hillsides dotted with yellow and magenta blossoms from prickly pear and pincushion cactus. Sharp cactus spines aren't the only things you have to watch for; the Red Deer Forks is a prime area for prairie rattlesnakes.

ABOVE: *Pincushion cactus.*
BELOW: *Prickly pear cactus.*

ABOVE: *Rugged hills along the South Saskatchewan River near the Red Deer River Forks.*

OPPOSITE: *The South Saskatchewan River Valley near the Lemsford Ferry.*

OPPOSITE: *South Saskatchewan River near Batoche.*

ABOVE: *Saskatchewan River Forks east of Prince Albert, where the South and North Saskatchewan Rivers meet.*

Qu'Appelle Valley

Formed some 14,000 years ago, the Qu'Appelle Valley is one of the widest, longest and deepest glacial spillways on the prairies, providing a dramatic contrast to the plains on either side. The valley begins to take shape at Lake Diefenbaker where the Qu'Appelle River originates. Twisting and turning across the wide valley bottom, the river flows for about 500 kilometres, more than halfway across Saskatchewan, eventually joining the Assiniboine River just across the border into Manitoba. Because of its shallow gradient, the river is usually a quiet meandering stream, except during run-off when it periodically floods.

The gentle beauty of the valley changes from west to east. In the western portion, steep hills are covered with mixed grasses on drier south-facing slopes, while stands of moisture-loving ash, Manitoba maple and aspen thrive on shadier north-facing slopes. The forest on both sides of the valley becomes thicker in the eastern section which lies within the Aspen Parkland Ecoregion. A special feature of the eastern Qu'Appelle is stands of bur oak, the most northerly of North American oak trees.

OPPOSITE: *The slopes of the Qu'Appelle Valley near Crooked Lake.*
RIGHT: *The Qu'Appelle River.*

Throughout the Qu'Appelle Valley, the river's broad flood plain is interspersed with pasture, cropland, large lakes and small wetlands.

Along its course, the Qu'Appelle River widens into lakes including Eyebrow and Buffalo Pound Lakes in the west, and Round Lake and Crooked Lake in the east. Between them is a chain of four lakes known as the Fishing Lakes – Pasqua, Echo, Mission, and Katepwa – separated by deposits of sand, gravel and silt carried by tributaries emptying into the river.

It's a valley whose beauty has inspired romantic legends. The classic poem by E. Pauline Johnson tells of young man making his way across a lake to claim his bride. Twice he heard his name called, to which he answered in French, *Qu'Appelle?* or "Who calls?" Reaching his lover's camp, he found death fires burning on shore, and knew immediately that his bride had died. It was then that he realized that it was her voice he had heard, calling out across the still night just as the moon rose.

ABOVE: *The Qu'Appelle River and its broad flood plain.*
OPPOSITE: *Katepwa Lake in the Qu'Appelle Valley.*

Little bluestem, a native grass, turns a reddish hue in early fall, adding color to these hills in the Qu'Appelle Valley.

Souris River Valley

The Souris River flows through Weyburn, widens into Rafferty Reservoir, then meanders east through Estevan, Roche Percee and Oxbow before turning south into North Dakota. Originating as a major glacial spillway that deeply entrenched the plains, the broad Souris Valley now appears overly large for the narrow twisting river. While sections of the fertile river flats are used for crops or hay, pastureland with native grasses covers much of the steep and often stony valley slopes.

Some stretches of the Souris River are lined with stands of aspen, ash, elm and Manitoba maple which form a tunnel-like canopy over the narrow river, while open grassland with few trees covers neighboring hillsides. The plantlife has a lot in common with that in landscapes farther southeast. As a result, the valley is home to numerous plants considered rare in Saskatchewan. Many species reach their northern or western limits here.

Our favorite stretch of the valley is in the Roche Percee area east of Estevan where the valley slopes are lined with strangely-shaped weathered sandstone outcroppings, cliffs and hoodoos. The best known formation is Roche Percee, an imposing hilltop outcropping that once had a window-like hole, hence the French name *roche percée* meaning "pierced rock". Aboriginal people,

Souris River between Roche Percee and Oxbow.

who left offerings at its base, were the first to etch designs in the easily-worked soft sandstone. Later the rock became a landmark for North West Mounted Police patrols and settlers who carved their names in the rock. Although the upper part of the pierced rock has long since collapsed, it remains a prominent landmark.

The most intriguing sandstone formations are on private pastures on either side of the valley, especially those in the pasture of the

Parent family who also operate Happy Valley Bed and Breakfast. The Parents have even built a path where guests can walk to explore the fascinating cliffs, ledges protruding over a deep ravine, pierced rocks and pock-marked hoodoos.

ABOVE AND LEFT: *Mother Nature may have been in a whimsical mood in the Souris Valley, creating strange but delightful sandstone formations.*
OPPOSITE: *Sandstone formations line the Souris Valley east of Roche Percee.*

ABOVE AND OPPOSITE: *Sandstone formations east of Roche Percee in the Souris Valley.*

The approach to Herbert Ferry Regional Park on the south shore of Lake Diefenbaker.

The Great Prairie Lake

When Gardiner Dam was completed in 1967, an enormous section of the South Saskatchewan River was flooded, creating Lake Diefenbaker. It is now the largest body of fresh water in southern Saskatchewan, with close to 800 kilometres of shoreline.

While the lake itself has artificial origins, much of the surrounding terrain remains in a natural state. Indeed, the vast tract of rangeland on the north shore which belonged to the great Matador Ranch in the early 1900s, is considered one of the last large uncultivated areas of native prairie on clay soils left in the Northern Plains.

ABOVE: *Coyotes are common in the hills bordering Lake Diefenbaker.*
RIGHT: *Richardson's ground squirrels, commonly referred to as gophers, sound an alarm when danger is near.*

All of the provincial and regional parks surrounding Lake Diefenbaker offer commanding views of the lake and countryside. Among our favorites is the awe-inspiring approach to Saskatchewan Landing Provincial Park on the west end of the lake. South of Kyle on Highway #4, the mostly level farmland suddenly drops into the deep broad valley, with sweeping views over the sharply sculpted ridges, vast stretches of native grasslands, wooded coulees and protected bays.

More incredible views are in store along the Coulee Trail, hiking up Brunyee Ridge, or just wandering in the hills where cactus blooms on the grassy slopes and majestic cottonwoods cluster around a moist creek bed. The strong scent of sage and the sweet smell of wolf willow and juniper blend into a distinctive prairie fragrance.

The varied habitats support wildlife such as mule deer, white-tailed deer, coyotes and pronghorn antelope, along with a wide array of waterfowl, songbirds and raptors. Rarities include yellow-breasted chats, lark sparrows and long-billed curlews.

ABOVE: *The hills of Saskatchewan Landing Provincial Park.*
OPPOSITE: *Swift Current Creek begins in the north slopes of the Cypress Hills, winds its way northeast through the city of Swift Current, then empties into the south shore of Lake Diefenbaker. In the last few kilometres south* *of the lake, the creek cuts through a deep rugged valley. Private pastureland extends through the valley and, except for roaming cattle, the native prairie remains relatively undisturbed. The view here is where the grid road east of Stewart Valley crosses Swift Current Creek.*

OPPOSITE: *The Sand Castle southwest of Beechy is a steeply-sloped hogs-back with castle-like spires, deeply etched eroded banks and cracked and baked fragile soil. The entire area around the Sand Castle is breathtaking. The trail in follows the rim of the valley, with commanding views along the* shoreline and across the lake. This wild country of cactus, sage, wolf willow, bull snakes and long-billed curlews is also prime nesting territory for prairie falcons and golden eagles.

ABOVE: *Hills on the north shore of Lake Diefenbaker near the Sand Castle.*

Prairie Wetlands

Lakeshore, marshes, sloughs, ponds and potholes. While they come in different sizes and shapes and go by different names, wetlands rank among the most significant parts of the Saskatchewan landscape.

Saskatchewan wetlands are important to North America and, indeed, to the entire western hemisphere. Saskatchewan is called "North America's duck factory" since as many as one in four ducks on the continent is raised here. The province has a quarter of the world's white pelicans, about a fifth of North America's piping plovers, and one of the largest inland concentrations of bald eagles. Over half of North America's snow geese, sandhill cranes, whooping cranes, sanderlings and Hudsonian godwits stop in Saskatchewan during migration.

OPPOSITE: *Snow geese at Luck Lake during fall migration.*
RIGHT: *An American bittern near Last Mountain Lake.*

Special wetlands are many. In 1887, the first bird sanctuary in North America was established at Last Mountain Lake. The National Wildlife Area at the north end of the lake, also designated a Wetland of International Importance, provides a haven for 280 resident and migratory bird species including rarities such as peregrine falcons and whooping cranes.

Canada's largest saline lakes, the Quill Lakes – Big Quill, Middle Quill, and Little Quill – are among the most important wetlands in the western hemisphere. Over 300,000 migrating shorebirds, such as sanderlings, dowitchers, red-necked phalaropes, semipalmated and stilt sandpipers, and Hudsonian godwits stop at these saline lakes and adjoining freshwater marshes on their annual migration. Many nest in the Canadian Arctic, then travel as far south as South America. The shallow mudflats on the shores of the Quill Lakes have an abundant supply of invertebrates such as midge larvae, which the birds eat to replenish their

fat reserves for the next leg of their marathon journey.

Because of their critical role, the Quill Lakes were recognized in 1994 as part of the Western Hemisphere Shorebird Reserve Network which extends from Canada to Argentina. The rich food supply also attracts nesting shorebirds such as the American avocet, killdeer, common snipe, marbled godwit, and endangered piping plover.

Redberry Lake, along with its watershed, the community of Hafford, and much of the surrounding rural municipality, was the first area in Saskatchewan designated a World Biosphere Reserve by the United Nations. Redberry Lake is best known for the large colony of American white pelicans that nest on the islands. Once considered an endangered species, white pelicans have made a remarkable comeback, due in large part to the protection they have received in sanctuaries such as this.

Located in the Aspen Parkland Ecoregion, Redberry supports diverse wildlife including close to 200 bird species which either nest here or pass through during migration. The lake is home to piping plovers, as well as the largest concentration of nesting white-winged scoters in North America.

While Redberry Lake has a regional park and a small cottage community, it has been spared the over-development that has plagued some lakes. Nature still takes centre stage here. The Redberry Pelican Project

RIGHT: *Marbled godwit.*
OPPOSITE: *Mallard (top left), American avocet (top right), wood duck (bottom left). Birdwatchers on the south shore of Little Quill Lake (bottom right).*

and the Stuart Houston Ecology Centre at the park coordinate research projects as well as conduct ecotours to help visitors appreciate the lake and its wildlife. While the lake itself is the centrepiece of the World Biosphere Reserve, also important is the mosaic of natural aspen groves, wetlands and agricultural and grazing land in the surrounding area.

Nestled between Buffalo Pound Lake and the confluence of the Qu'Appelle and Moose Jaw Rivers, Nicolle Flats is one of few stretches of river flats in the Qu'Appelle Valley that is primarily native habitat.

Bordering the lake and marsh are valley slopes covered in native grasses and shrubs, and wooded coulees where green ash and Manitoba maple thrive in moister conditions. The diverse landscape in turn attracts diverse wildlife. Painted turtles bask in the sun on river mudflats and a freshwater spring lures kingbirds, eastern phoebe and other songbirds. Several species of waterfowl nest here, and gather in impressive numbers during fall migration. The lake is an important summering area for white pelicans and cormorants, and is site of what is believed to be the oldest great blue heron colony in continuous use in Saskatchewan.

Chaplin Lake, Luck Lake, and Foam Lake Marsh are only a few of Saskatchewan's other prominent wetlands. But just as important are the thousands of potholes and marshes that dot the prairie and parkland, many of which co-exist with farmland.

Wetlands have had a tough go of it over the years, with the perception that "better use" could be made of the land. Around 40% of Saskatchewan's wetlands are already gone. While the threat to wetlands has certainly not disappeared, at least now there is growing recognition of their importance and a concerted effort to save what remains.

OPPOSITE: *American white pelicans are the most famous residents of Redberry Lake.*
ABOVE: *Nicolle Flats Marsh, Buffalo Pound Provincial Park.*

Eastern Rivers and Forests

Duck Mountain Highlands

Travelling through the farmland east of Kamsack, you see the hills looming in the distance. As you get closer the farmland gives way to thick aspen woodlands dotted with tall white spruce, balsam poplar and birch. After climbing over 200 metres, you enter a completely different environment that is cooler and moister than the plains below. The Duck Mountain Highlands are the southern extent of the boreal forest in Saskatchewan, a place that seems like it should be much farther north, yet its latitude is actually farther south than Saskatoon.

OPPOSITE: *Little Boggy Creek.*
RIGHT: *Marsh marigolds.*

The highlands are part of the Manitoba Escarpment that extends over western Manitoba and a portion of eastern Saskatchewan. The hills consist of a thick layer of some 200 metres of glacial till deposited when the last glaciers stopped migrating southward and began to melt where they were, leaving behind massive amounts of silt, gravel and sand.

Ponds are common, creating wetlands that attract a variety of wildlife from great blue herons and osprey to moose, elk and black bear. The largest body of water is Madge Lake, a focal point for Duck Mountain Provincial Park. Madge Lake and water bodies in the north drain towards the Swan River which empties into the Saskatchewan River, while the southern area drains into Little Boggy Creek which flows into the

Assiniboine River. Both river systems flow into Lake Winnipeg and eventually into Hudson Bay.

Our favorite area is in the southern hills around Little Boggy Creek, a narrow waterway that meanders through dense forest, its banks alive with bright yellow marsh marigolds in early summer. This idyllic place is set against the backdrop of forested hills, with grassy meadows above the creek sprinkled with three-flowered avens, hoary puccoons, yarrow and the blue blossoms of lungwort.

ABOVE: *The Ski Hill Road in Duck Mountain Provincial Park.*
OPPOSITE: *The Barrier River begins in the hills south of Melfort and empties into the Red Deer River in the Greenwater Lake area. Along its* *course it widens into two long narrow lakes – Kipabiskau Lake, site of a regional park, and Barrier Lake. The section of river shown here is just east of Kipabiskau Regional Park.*

A thick stand of ostrich ferns close to two metres high carpets the elm forest floor on the flood plain of the Red Deer River.

Red Deer River

The Red Deer River begins in the hills of the Greenwater Lake area, winds northeast to Hudson Bay and eventually empties into Red Deer Lake about 20 kilometres past the Manitoba border.

The river is lined with thick mixed wood forest of white and black spruce, balsam poplar, jack pine, aspen, green ash, Manitoba maple and American elm. The most fascinating sections are where periodic flooding has created ideal conditions for almost pure stands of elm. One of these is the Rendek Elm Forest, a beautiful natural riverside property owned and protected by Nature Saskatchewan.

In another spot, gigantic elms, many close to a metre in diameter, form a high closed forest canopy. Carpeting the forest floor are luxuriant stands of ostrich ferns, which in mid-summer grow close to two metres high. Elm trees release a chemical growth inhibitor which decreases competition from other plants on the forest floor. However, ostrich ferns are immune, and thrive in the shady environment.

To photograph the ferns, we had to wait for calm cloudy conditions so that the ferns would stay still and the light under the forest canopy would be evenly diffused. Early one July evening when the elements

The Red Deer River northeast of Hudson Bay.

cooperated, we descended the ridge into the enchanted forest below. It was like entering another world. The stillness, heat and humidity weighed heavily with every step, and a sweet pungent odor permeated the air. The sensation was immediately familiar; it felt exactly like being in a tropical rainforest.

It was one of those defining moments that really brought home what a marvelously diverse province this is. The week before we were in southern badlands where the relentless sun parched the land, drought resistant plants fought for survival, and the constant wind dried and burned our skin. A few days later, and not too far away, we stood in an emerald green jungle.

Rice River Canyon

It was a backpacking trip into a spectacular river valley. Steep canyon walls were covered in thick forest, except where landslides had collapsed the soft banks. The ice-cold river was laden with silt as it raced over massive boulders. Uprooted trees were scattered like match sticks, remnants of powerful spring floods. Muddy banks revealed tracks of wolf, moose, woodland caribou and cougar.

The Rice River Canyon slices through the Pasquia Hills, about 80 kilometres north of Hudson Bay. The river flows for only about 20 kilometres before emptying into the Carrot River, but in that short distance it has carved a canyon thought to be the steepest anywhere in Saskatchewan. In a nine kilometre stretch, the river drops 350 metres, or over 1,100 feet.

Our trip into the canyon was led by David Weiman of Sawyer Lake Adventures. We approached the headwaters of the Rice River from the east, first travelling part way down a logging road by four-wheel drive truck, then walking along a winter logging

OPPOSITE AND RIGHT: *Iron-rich groundwater seeping from an eroded bank of the Rice River slowly evaporates, staining the rocks and soil blood red.*

trail. In spring the trail turns wet, so more often than not we slogged through bog or mud, each step taking twice the effort as our feet stuck in the ooze and muck.

After about eight kilometres of walking, mostly uphill, David smiled as he announced that the easy part was over. We were only three kilometres from the edge of the canyon, but the rest of the way was bushwhacking through thick forest. Taking a compass bearing, we headed into the bush, picking our way through a maze of fallen trees that had lost their protection from the wind when the adjacent forest was clear-cut. We constantly had to be careful of our footing in the spongy mats of moss, pools of open water and groves of tangled alder.

A short scramble down the steep forested hillside brought us into the canyon. The setting was breathtaking – a deep narrow valley with a small rushing stream. The riverbed was cluttered with massive white spruce, scattered and sometimes piled high as if pushed by a bulldozer. We were forced to climb over these giant pick-up sticks and, where our route was blocked, we had to cross the river by hopping over rounded boulders.

Further downstream the canyon quickly became deeper and steeper. In one place a large landslide had swept away all vegetation and much of the soil. Rocks and soil on

the river's edge were blood red, a result of iron-rich groundwater oozing from the eroded bank and slowly evaporating, leaving red deposits.

The Rice River Canyon is more than spectacular scenery. What impressed us most was that this was still an undisturbed wilderness, governed by nature's rhythms. We were less than a half day's walk from the road, yet we had a feeling of being somewhere much more remote, where few people have ventured and with no signs of "civilization". We couldn't help but wonder how much longer it will be possible to experience wilderness this far south in Saskatchewan.

ABOVE: *Iron-stained rocks and soil.*
OPPOSITE: *The confluence of two major tributaries of the Rice River.*

Heading Northwest

Manitou Sand Hills

As you drive along Highway #40 close to the Alberta border, the gently rolling farmland gives no hint of the dramatically different terrain just a few kilometres to the south. The Manitou Sand Hills cover more than 53,000 hectares or 130,000 acres of hilly grasslands, wooded valleys and wetlands. Because of the rugged landscape and dry sandy soil, this vast tract of land has never been broken for agriculture. It's considered the largest area of relatively undisturbed native vegetation in the Aspen Parkland Ecoregion of Saskatchewan.

Besides large, saline Manitou Lake, several smaller lakes, marshes and springs are

OPPOSITE: *John Graham leads a horseback trek through the Manitou Sand Hills.*
RIGHT: *Western red lily, Saskatchewan's floral emblem.*

scattered throughout the hills. An unusual feature is that saline and fresh bodies of water are found next to each other, resulting in a rich diversity of landforms and wildlife. In some places the plantlife is more typical of the boreal forest while in others it's more like the southern grasslands. Scientists have identified around 400 plant species, nine of which are rare.

White-tailed deer and mule deer often dart out of the bushes, coyotes howl at night and soaring hawks ride the thermals. The birdlife is rich and varied with 145 species of waterfowl, shorebirds, songbirds and raptors. The wetlands are home to one of the larger populations of endangered piping plover, and are important to migratory shorebirds such as Wilson's phalarope and red-necked phalarope.

Most of the Manitou Sand Hills are Crown land divided into several grazing cooperatives. Here the horse is still king. Local farmer John Graham operates Manitou

Outfitters, taking guests on horseback treks through this natural prairie. Since the pastures are so large, you can ride all day without seeing a fence, other people, or any intrusion from the modern world, except cattle. Riding through these hills is to experience what much of the northern prairie was like before settlement.

To do the treks, John Graham quips that he has a horse for everyone. "For quiet people I have quiet horses. For fast people I have fast horses. For heavy people I have heavy horses. And for those who have never ridden a horse before, I even have horses that have never been ridden before."

ABOVE: *A peninsula in Manitou Lake.*
OPPOSITE: *A delightful walking trail leads through thick forest at Brightsand Lake Regional Park east of St. Walburg. Offering incredible* *variety, the trail system includes high eskers, fens, marshlands, black spruce and tamarack lowlands, white spruce highlands, grassy meadows, and lakefront beach ridges.*

North of Loon Lake, the Beaver River quietly winds eastward across the undulating landscape. The gently sloping valley was formed by the tremendous volume of glacial meltwater that poured into Glacial Meadow Lake some 12,000 years ago. The peaceful river is now a meandering stream with broad loops, oxbow lakes, abandoned channels and embankments that have built up from sediment deposited during periods of high run-off.

Meadow Lake Provincial Park

On Saskatchewan's western border and midway up the province, Meadow Lake Provincial Park marks a transition. For the most part, Saskatchewan's agricultural land reaches its northern limit just south of here. The 1,600 square kilometre park includes a rich variety of boreal forest ecosystems – jack pine on dry sandy soil, large stands of aspen, birch and spruce, and lush green carpets of moss in tamarack bogs and black spruce forest. This is ideal habitat for moose, elk, white-tailed deer, black bear, and numerous forest-nesting birds such as white-throated sparrows, woodpeckers, owls, bald eagles and warblers.

Meadow Lake is one of the most popular provincial parks in Saskatchewan, with forest trails for pleasant hikes, and rivers and lakes for fishing and canoeing. The landscape was reworked by glaciers that laid down layers of silt, sand and gravel, carried huge boulders from the Canadian Shield far to the north, and left behind long ridges of sand eskers. Many smaller lakes originated as blocks of breakaway glacial ice that became embedded in the sand, forming lakes as they melted.

While over 200,000 people visit the park each year, it's easy to find beautiful natural

The Newbranch Hiking Trail in Meadow Lake Provincial Park takes you through forest and lakelands and over eskers. Here, the trail overlooks the creek between Peitahigan Lake and Third Mustus Lake.

areas with no one else around, especially if you go hiking or canoeing. One warm summer's day we canoed through the series of Mustus Lakes which are immensely popular for fishing. At the end of Third Mustus Lake, we entered a narrow, barely navigable creek flowing from Peitahigan Lake. It immediately became more peaceful as we left the motorboats behind and followed the meandering creek through high reeds and a secluded wetland full of waterfowl. Just

ahead of us a merganser sat on her crudely built floating nest. A pair of belted kingfishers flitted from one tree to another along the shore. A white-tailed deer and her fawn peered out from the bushes. A great blue heron stood motionless like a statue on the water's edge. We hadn't travelled far, yet it seemed like we had entered a different world.

Prince Albert National Park in the fall.

The Lakelands

Wanderings in Grey Owl Country

Grey Owl called Prince Albert National Park "one of Canada's greatest wilderness playgrounds". Easy to reach and easy to connect with, this is Saskatchewan's accessible wilderness.

The park covers 3,875 square kilometres, or about a million acres of wilderness almost smack in the geographic centre of Saskatchewan. The park preserves a transition area between the aspen parkland of the south and the northern boreal forest. The southwest corner of the park also protects about one-third of Canada's remaining fescue grasslands.

Dividing the park are the Waskesiu Hills, created from deposits left by glaciers some 10,000 years ago, and which now form the height of land between the Churchill River drainage system to the north and the Saskatchewan River system to the south. Because of this "inconvenient" location between two watersheds, the park area remained relatively untouched during the early years of the fur trade.

Water covers almost 30% of the park, with 1,500 lakes including large bodies of water such as Waskesiu, Kingsmere and Crean Lakes, among the largest in any of Canada's national parks. Towering white spruce, some of the tallest in the province, alternate with islands of jack pine, open aspen forest, marshy wetlands, low-lying bogs and grassy meadows.

The patchwork of vegetation brings diverse wildlife. Typical of the southern parkland are coyote, badger, elk and white-tailed deer, while black bear, moose, woodland caribou and wolf are typical of the northern forest. The park is also home to a herd of free-ranging plains bison, and to one of Canada's largest nesting colonies of American white pelicans, numbering about 15,000.

Canadian Tiger Swallowtail butterfly.

Hiking trails, canoe routes and places to escape into the backcountry abound. Among our favorites is the trip to Grey Owl's cabin, where a 20-kilometre hike, or canoe trip of about the same length, leads to tiny Ajawaan Lake, and the simple log cabin where Grey Owl wrote classics such as *Pilgrims of the Wild* and *Tales of an Empty Cabin* during the 1930s.

Several lakes outside the park have natural areas to explore. A good example is Anglin Lake, famous for its high population of resident loons, and its network of walking trails.

ABOVE: *White-tailed deer fawn.*
RIGHT: *Grey Owl's cabin on the shore of Ajawaan Lake is an idyllic spot to linger awhile and reflect on the legacy of this remarkable though controversial character. An Englishman masquerading as an Indian, he brought a message of respect for the natural world which was years ahead of its time – "Remember you belong to nature, not it to you."*
OPPOSITE: *The Narrows Hiking Trail, Prince Albert National Park.*

OPPOSITE: *Moss carpets the black spruce forest along a section of the Homestead Heritage Forest Trail near Candle Lake.*

ABOVE: *Steepbank Lake, part of Clarence/Steepbank Provincial Wilderness Park, is north of Candle Lake.*

ABOVE: *Fall colors on the shore of Steepbank Lake.*
OPPOSITE: *Jade Lake, one of the Gem Lakes.*

Gems in the Forest

Jade. Opal. Diamond. Sapphire. Pearl. These gemstones are scattered in the forest on the west end of Narrow Hills Provincial Park. The Gem Lakes originated in an extensive system of tunnel valleys that formed when meltwater flowed beneath the glacial ice, causing erosion. The valleys filled with a deep layer of sand deposits. Large pieces of ice embedded in the sand melted, forming kettle depressions that filled with water.

The lakes are small but deep. About 100 metres wide and a little over 200 metres long, Opal Lake is the smallest, yet it is over 20 metres deep. Although the lakes are very close together, they aren't connected by drainage channels; they are kept filled by water percolating up from the water table.

The lakes are surrounded by a mixed forest of white and black spruce, jack pine, aspen, balsam fir and birch, with shrubs around the edges. A walking trail follows the hilly land between the lakes, providing some striking views, but what's really special is the color. The depth of the water, the sandy bottom, and the surrounding vegetation give the lakes the ability to reflect lustrous blues and greens that seem unreal. If you happen to walk the trails when the water is calm, the air is clear, and the sunlight is just right, these tiny lakes truly do glisten like gemstones.

OPPOSITE: *Pearl Lake, one of the most colorful of the Gem Lakes.*

ABOVE: *Star trail at the Gem Lakes. A two-hour time exposure makes the stars look like streaks of light circling around the North Star. The trees were "painted" with a flashlight for about one minute to illuminate them.*

ABOVE AND OPPOSITE: *Driving along Highway #165 southeast of La Ronge, there's no hint of anything unusual as you cross the forest-fringed Nipekamew River. A narrow trail just east of the river leads you upstream through mixed woods of jack pine, black spruce and birch. Suddenly you emerge from the forest on the edge of a cliff where spires of brilliant white sand pillars rise some 23 metres from the river below. Sediments deposited here 120 million years ago have been eroded and exposed by the river that once had considerably more flow and force than it does today. Consisting mostly of medium to coarse grain sandstone, these fragile formations have been sculpted into delicate shapes and contours.*

90

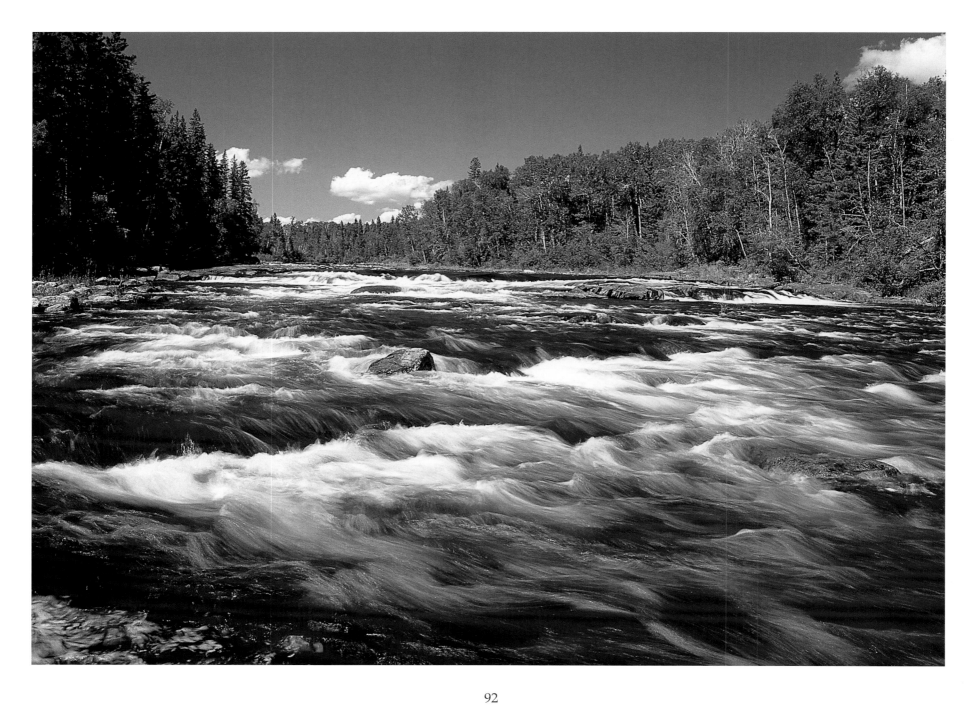

Churchill River Country

The Churchill River, in many ways, embodies the essence of northern Saskatchewan. Its rich history dates to the glory years of northern exploration, voyageurs and fur brigades, and even further back to when aboriginal people painted pictographs on the river's rocky ledges and cliffs. Today it is the most accessible of the great northern rivers, tailor-made for fishing, camping, exploring and simply experiencing the beauty of nature.

The Churchill River is essentially a series of island-studded lakes separated by rapids and waterfalls. For most of its length, the river flows through the aptly named Churchill River Upland Ecoregion, classic

OPPOSITE: *Great Devil Rapids on the Churchill River.*
RIGHT: *Pictographs near Stanley Rapids on the Churchill River.*

Precambrian Shield country with forested hills dotted with numerous clear lakes, massive outcroppings and cliffs of glacial sculpted bedrock. Only the extreme western stretch of the river, close to its headwaters near the Alberta border, lies outside the Shield.

Above all, this is quintessential canoe country with endless possibilities for exploring the river itself as well as the mind-boggling network of northern waterways joining the Churchill. A river of many faces, the Churchill can be a wild whitewater adventure or a gentle journey along placid lakes.

Paddling the Churchill is partly a connection to the past and partly a way to get in touch with the simple pleasures of nature's rhythms. The Churchill experience is freshly caught fish sizzling over a campfire, swimming in cool clear water on a hot summer afternoon, or finding that perfect wilderness campsite where, at the end of the day, the tangerine sun dips into a quiet lake. It's where the loudest sounds are the thunder of rapids and the haunting cry of a loon. It's where, at least for the present, all seems well with the world.

OPPOSITE: *Hayman Lake on the Churchill River.*

ABOVE: *Nistowiak Falls, where water from Iskwatikan Lake flows to Nistowiak Lake on the Churchill River system.*

OPPOSITE: *Northern lights over Drope Lake on the Churchill River.*

ABOVE: *Cumulonimbus mammatus clouds, commonly associated with thunderstorms, formed intriguing bubble-like shapes over Little Deer Lake north of La Ronge.*

Clearwater River

Hiking the Methye Portage.

Only a few days into our canoe trip, it became obvious why the Clearwater was declared a Canadian Heritage River. It has everything – stunning scenery, a rich history, and an exciting mix of exhilarating whitewater and peaceful stretches that add up to an exceptional canoe journey.

Part of the Arctic watershed, the Clearwater River begins at Broach Lake in northwest Saskatchewan, flows southeast, then makes an abrupt turn west, eventually joining the Athabasca River at Fort McMurray, Alberta. The upper section flows through Canadian Shield country characterized by huge outcroppings of Precambrian bedrock. Closer to the Alberta border, the river leaves the Shield and enters the Boreal Plain characterized by younger sedimentary rocks and soil and material deposited by glaciers.

OPPOSITE: *Clearwater River.*

Upstream, the riverbanks are low for the most part, interspersed with dramatic stretches such as imposing rock-lined Granite Gorge, and the Virgin River which pours out of Careen Lake just before joining the Clearwater. Further downstream, we paddled through long stretches of rock gardens with boulders the size of trucks, and portaged around canyons and waterfalls. We descended deeper and deeper into a valley formed by a glacial meltwater channel as large as any in Saskatchewan, and one of the most northerly. The wildest and most beautiful section of the 360-kilometre long river was between the confluence of the Descharme River and Contact Rapids, where it was one drop after another over rapids and waterfalls.

The Saskatchewan section of the Clearwater is protected as a Provincial Wilderness Park. The few visitors it sees each year are a far cry from 200 years ago when the lower section of the river was a major thoroughfare for the fur trade.

The key to this route was the famous Methye Portage, a 20-kilometre trail connecting the north end of Lac La Loche to the Clearwater River. An important aboriginal travel route for hundreds of years, the Methye Portage changed the face of the fur trade when Peter Pond discovered it in 1778. Also referred to as Portage La Loche, the trail provided a land bridge between the Churchill River system that drains eastward to Hudson Bay, and waterways draining to the Arctic Ocean. Pond's use of this route opened up the lucrative Athabasca country to the fur trade. For more than a century the portage was like a highway, first to voyageurs lugging furs and canoes, and later to York boat brigades hauling furs and supplies using horse and ox carts.

Travellers on the historic route read like a who's who of the fur trade and northern exploration – Alexander Mackenzie, Peter Fidler, Philip Turnor, David Thomson, John Franklin, George Back, among many others. To the ordinary men of the fur trade, crossing the Methye Portage was a rite of passage, where the novice *mangeur de lard* or pork-eater, became an *homme du nord*, a man of the north.

We couldn't help but feel a strong link to the past when we hiked the portage. Deep ruts spoke of thousands of footsteps and fur-laden carts. The only difficult section of trail was near the Lac La Loche end where we slogged through muskeg then waded thigh-deep through a creek flooded by a beaver dam. A kaleidoscope of boreal forest habitats followed – jack pine, white spruce, black spruce, balsam poplar, balsam fir, aspen, birch, muskeg and even pockets of grassland. It was early September and we gorged ourselves on blueberries at every rest stop.

After walking 13 kilometres, we arrived at Rendevous Lake (the official spelling of the lake's name omits the usual "z" in *rendezvous*), a small beautiful sandy lake where fur brigades from the north and the south met to exchange their loads. The trail, which so far had been fairly level, began a steep descent at the rim of the Clearwater Valley. At one spot the thick forest parted just enough to provide a magnificent view of

Running the rapids through Granite Gorge on the Clearwater River.

the three-kilometre wide valley, with the meandering river close to 200 metres below.

A common thread in the journals of the explorers was their impassioned description of this view. Franklin called it "the most picturesque and romantic prospect we had yet seen in this country." The great Arctic explorer George Back wrote of the reaction of his men upon reaching the valley rim. "Even the most jaded of the party, as he broke from the gloom of the wood on this enchanting scene, seemed to forget his weariness, and halted involuntarily with his burden, to gaze for a moment, with a sort of wondering admiration, on a spectacle so novel and magnificent."

Contact Rapids, Clearwater River.

ABOVE AND OPPOSITE: *Skull Canyon, Clearwater River.*

Athabasca Country

Athabasca Sand Dunes

Saskatchewan's most exotic landscape is in a class by itself – the largest active sand fields in Canada, the most northerly major dunes in the world, a desert-like environment strangely misplaced in the northern forest. The Athabasca Sand Dunes stretch for about 100 kilometres along the south shore of Lake Athabasca, and are part of the Athabasca Plains Ecoregion where a thick layer of sandstone covers the underlying bedrock.

A Dene legend tells of a giant beaver speared by a hunter. In the throes of death, the beaver kicked up the soil to such an extent that it was ground into sand. Scientists have a more complex explanation involving the retreat of glaciers, sandstone sediment deposited in deltas, and strong

OPPOSITE: *The knife-edge crest of a giant dune in the William River Dune Field.*

winds whipping the sand into dunes after the water receded.

Canoeing the William River, the main waterway running through the dunes, was like travelling along a narrow ribbon dividing two dramatically different worlds. The east bank was covered in jack pine forest typical of the north, but to the west we could see only massive sand banks rising as much as 30 metres from the water's edge. For most of its length, the William is lined with stretch after stretch of rapids and rock gardens. Then 18 kilometres before it empties into Lake Athabasca, the William becomes so choked with sand that this raging river suddenly widens into a quiet, meandering braided stream, clogged with sand bars, with no rocks anywhere in sight.

West of the William River lie 40 or so giant dunes. Rising from a mostly level sandy plain to as much as 35 metres, some of these monsters are over a kilometre long. Strong opposing winds from the west and east

Two endemic plants, felt-leafed willow (right) and floccose tansy (front), growing with fireweed.

helped shape these dunes, giving the largest ones sharp knife-edge crests that flow in sinuous curves.

Most intriguing are the exhumed forests. Originally buried hundreds of years ago by moving sand, these ancient trees have more recently been exhumed from their sandy tomb as the dunes continued their eastward migration with the prevailing winds. A ghostly whitish-gray by day, these contorted skeletons seem to take on a new life as the evening sun bathes them in a warm red glow.

Athabasca Sand Dunes was declared a Provincial Wilderness Park for its unique plant life as much as for its spectacular scenery. Over 300 plants grow here, 52 of which are considered rare in Saskatchewan. Ten of these – five broad leaved herbs, four willows and one grass – are endemic, meaning that they occur nowhere else in the world. Why Athabasca is so rich in endemic plants is an evolutionary puzzle not yet solved.

There is more to Athabasca's south shore than sand dunes. To the east is the MacFarlane River, at its most dramatic just before emptying into Lake Athabasca where it plunges over a series of waterfalls then skirts the eastern edge of the sand dunes.

Farther east, the Otherside River rushes over a long stretch of rapids before reaching Otherside Bay on Lake Athabasca. The bay is home to Otherside River Lodge, run by Cliff and Stella Blackmur who have introduced us to many of the wonders of the northland. Most guests come for trophy pike and lake trout catch-and-release fishing. For us this special place has always meant adventure, a comfortable base to start and end our Athabasca explorations.

OPPOSITE: *The sand-clogged William River, seen from the air.*
ABOVE: *A towering wall of sand on the west bank of the William River.*
RIGHT: *Colorful lichens along a walking trail near Otherside River Lodge.*

ABOVE: *An exhumed forest in Thomson Bay on the south shore of Lake Athabasca.*

OPPOSITE: *The MacFarlane River plunges over a series of waterfalls and rapids before reaching the south shore of Lake Athabasca.*

Grandeur of the North Shore

Everything about Lake Athabasca is grand. Covering 7,850 square kilometres, Saskatchewan's largest lake is also the fourth largest lake entirely within Canada and the ninth largest lake in North America. The north and south shores are like two different worlds; long sweeping sandy beaches and dunes of the south shore give way to rocky outcroppings, deep bays, long peninsulas and innumerable islands on the north shore.

Special places are everywhere, like the falls at the mouth of the Bulyea River, hidden in a bay within a bay near the mouth of the Grease River. Or MacIntosh Bay, its narrow entrance opening into a broad inlet surrounded by immense hills ranging from nearly vertical rock walls with sparse vegetation to densely forested bulbous hills.

It's a delight to travel by boat or canoe along the north shore where the many bays, channels and islands hold hidden secrets. On one trip, we came out of a protected channel between Moose Island and the mainland to find the lake swells too high for comfort. Looking for somewhere to land and wait it out (something we do a lot on this lake), we found an inviting beach formed entirely of pebbles with a slight purple tinge. Behind

ABOVE AND OPPOSITE: *Cliffs of Reed Bay.*

the beach, the stones were lichen-encrusted where the land rose gradually into a series of ancient beach ridges showing former levels of Lake Athabasca.

Beaverlodge Mountain dominates the north shore. According to Dene legend, this was home to the mythical giant beaver that helped shape the land by damming the huge lake and thrashing the south shore into sand. In the middle of the bay lies Beaverlodge Island, said to contain the secret entrance to a tunnel beneath the lake,

where the giant beaver once escaped from a hunter.

The most dramatic setting is Reed Bay, its eastern shore lined with perfectly vertical cliffs rising straight from the deep water. The odd tree clings precariously to life and brightly colored lichen blankets weathered rock faces. While beautiful anytime, at sunset you could swear that the cliffs were made of gold.

ABOVE: *Bulbous hills bordering MacIntosh Bay.*
OPPOSITE: *A pebble beach on Lake Athabasca's north shore.*

The maze of islands stretching from the end of the Crackingstone
Peninsula almost half way across Lake Athabasca to the south shore
were the most fascinating to explore. Large forested islands contrasted
with smaller ones of pure rock where nature had carved and painted
complex abstract patterns.

ABOVE: Intriguing examples of ancient geological formations were
evident along wave-washed and glaciated rocky shorelines. Here on
Johnston Island, light-colored boulders in a red iron-rich matrix reveal
the structure of a two-billion-year-old basal conglomerate. We thought
it looked like a polished inlaid table top.
RIGHT: A cliff on Johnston Island is a deep red due to high iron
content in the rocks.

OPPOSITE: Part of this rocky cliff on the shore of Lodge Bay crumbled
eons ago, leaving boulders scattered along the hillside. One slender rock
pinnacle remains, standing as a lone sentinel keeping watch over this
bay of myths.

Far North

Hunt Falls

It seems fitting that Saskatchewan's highest waterfall is set in some of the most dramatic scenery in the province. Hunt Falls, also referred to as Lefty's Falls, is on the Grease River, about 40 kilometres northwest of Stony Rapids. In a single drop, the falls plunge 15 metres and form a cataract about 60 metres wide. Hunt Falls is part of a spectacular three-kilometre stretch where the river drops 35 metres.

The Grease is among the wildest rivers in the north, riddled with rapids, canyons and chutes. It flows south into Lake Athabasca, and is part of the Mackenzie River watershed that drains into the Arctic Ocean.

Our float plane landed above the falls on long narrow Eagle Rock Lake, named for bald eagles that nest on the cliffs. As we

OPPOSITE AND RIGHT : *Hunt Falls.*

followed the path over rocky outcroppings and through open jack pine forest, we could hear the roar grow increasingly louder with each step. Standing on the rocky ledge beside the brink of the falls, we could feel nature's immense power as the great wall of water thundered directly below us. In contrast, a delicate spray on the opposite bank drifted into the canyon, nourishing a unique mist meadow at the base of the falls.

Mosses and herbaceous plants thrive in the perpetually moist conditions, almost like a little tropical garden.

The entire setting is magnificent, with the river winding deeper into a broad green canyon. The northwest shore of Eagle Rock Lake is lined with vertical ridges rising as high as 50 metres, their bases littered with huge boulders that tumbled off eons ago.

What impressed us most about Hunt Falls was the feeling of solitude; being totally alone in a gorgeous wilderness that has seen little human impact and doesn't seem to be at risk, at least so far.

ABOVE AND OPPOSITE: *Grease River.*

Selwyn Lake
North and South of 60

As we flew northeast of Stony Rapids, the labyrinth of trees and water beneath us stretched to the horizon. Saskatchewan has close to 100,000 lakes, and from the window of the Single Otter float plane, it seemed as if we could see most of them.

The northeast corner of Saskatchewan is part of the Selwyn Lake Upland Ecoregion. Also called the Land of Little Sticks, this is a transition zone between the boreal forest and the tundra. Trees here are shorter and thinner, mostly widely spaced black spruce, with jack pine on drier ridges and sandy eskers, and a generous sprinkling of tamarack and birch. A kaleidoscope of colorful lichens and mosses carpets the forest floor. Boggy lowlands and mossy hummocks provide a spongy, springy feel to your step or, if you're not careful, a sudden sinking feeling!

Selwyn Lake straddles the 60th parallel, partly in Saskatchewan and partly in the Northwest Territories. Selwyn's octopus arms dangle in all directions, resulting in a bewildering maze of deep bays and inlets. Rugged forested hills blend with long sandy eskers, stony glacial deposits and rocky islands.

The float plane brought us to Common Island on the Saskatchewan side of the lake, home of Selwyn Lake Lodge, where visitors from around the world enjoy all the comforts of home while spending their days catch-and-release fishing for gigantic lake trout and northern pike. But there's more here than big fish. Owners Gord and Mary Wallace also take a keen interest in showing their guests the natural wonders and rich history of the great lake.

Selwyn Lake is remote even by today's standards, yet the Dene have been travelling these waterways for centuries, depending on the barren-ground caribou that migrate here every winter from their calving grounds in the tundra. Abandoned settlements, old cabins, and grave markers

ABOVE: *Colorful mosses cover the forest floor near Selwyn Lake.*
OPPOSITE: *The dock at Selwyn Lake Lodge.*

are scattered around the shore. Simply-built log cabins were shored with sand around the base to provide extra insulation, logs were chinked with moss, and log roofs were covered with a thick layer of moss and sand.

One day we stopped our boat at the base of a long esker, then climbed to the top for a better view over the lake. On the sandy hilltop clearing were the remains of an old campfire. At first we wondered why it was here, seemingly in the middle of nowhere, but after a closer look, the setting made sense. This esker overlooks a narrows in the lake, a natural funnel between high hills and a likely winter corridor for caribou – an ideal place for a hunter to wait.

Despite its enormous size, much of Selwyn Lake is protected by bays and islands, one reason why the Dene called this the Lake of Little Wind. There is one potentially treacherous crossing where travellers are exposed to a large expanse of open water, with one small island about halfway across. The story goes that an old shaman told his people that they would be guaranteed safe passage on this crossing if they buried him on the island.

The strangest story is that of Shaky Island. People have sworn that when they landed on the small rocky island, the ground began to shake as if in an earthquake. Some people still refuse to set foot there.

Most fascinating is the story of the Sacred Lake. At the northern end of Selwyn Lake, an old portage trail crosses a height of land to Flett Lake in the Northwest Territories. A short walk off the trail leads to a tiny hidden lake surrounded by trees and backed by a high vertical cliff. For as long as anyone can remember, this lake has been sacred to the Dene. When missionaries came, the church sent a bishop to bless the lake, which is regarded as having healing properties. Today it remains a place of pilgrimage for believers who come here because of personal afflictions or to take the special water back for family and friends.

ABOVE: *A sandy esker overlooking Selwyn Lake.*
OPPOSITE: *Selwyn Lake.*

Ecoregions of Saskatchewan

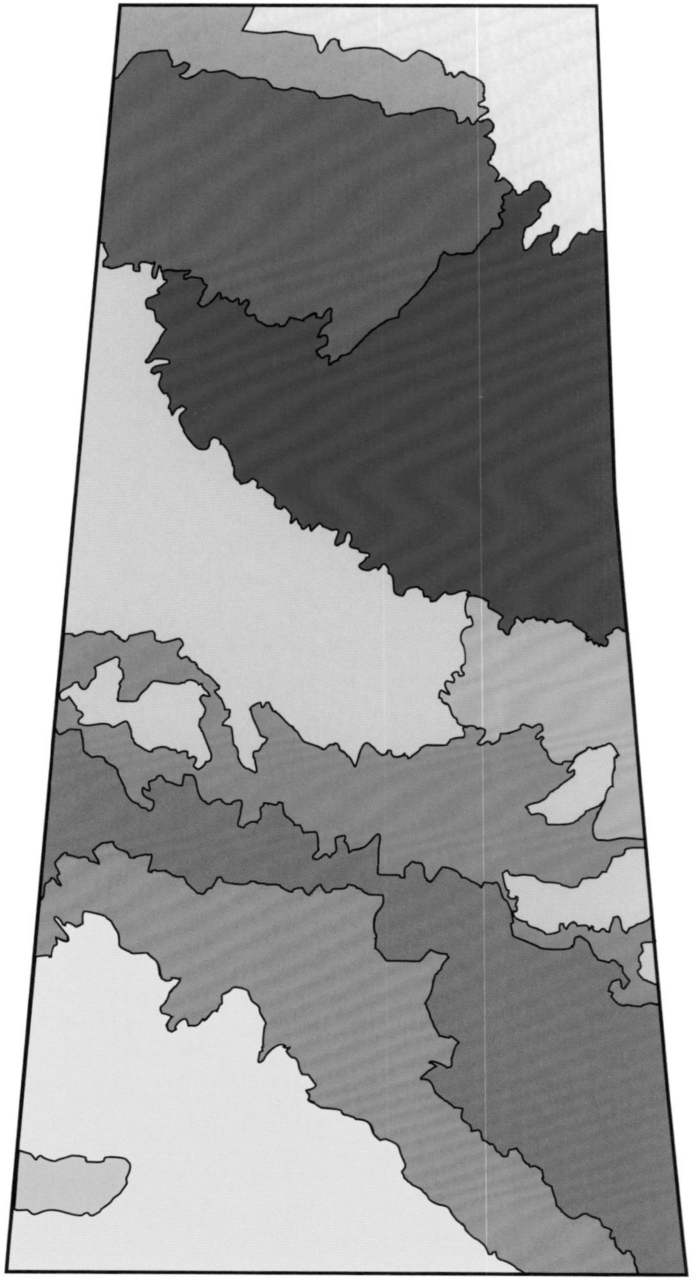

TAIGA SHIELD ECOZONE

Selwyn Lake Upland Ecoregion

Tazin Lake Upland Ecoregion

BOREAL SHIELD ECOZONE

Athabasca Plain Ecoregion

Churchill River Upland Ecoregion

BOREAL PLAIN ECOZONE

Mid-Boreal Upland Ecoregion

Mid-Boreal Lowland Ecoregion

Boreal Transition Ecoregion

PRAIRIE ECOZONE

Aspen Parkland Ecoregion

Moist Mixed Grassland Ecoregion

Mixed Grassland Ecoregion

Cypress Upland Ecoregion

Map produced by Parkland Publishing with permission from SPMC.

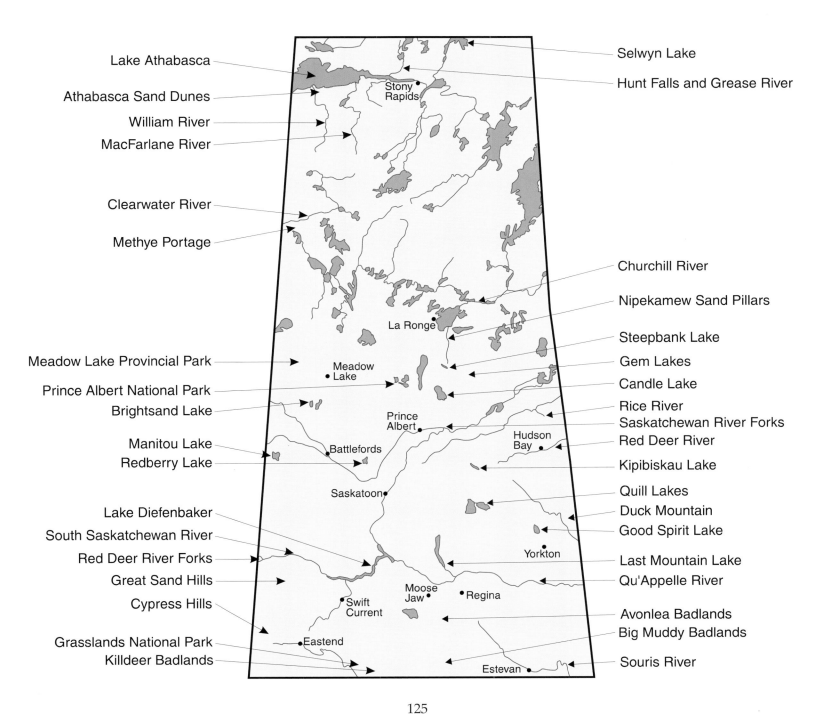

Lake Athabasca

Athabasca Sand Dunes

William River

MacFarlane River

Clearwater River

Methye Portage

Meadow Lake Provincial Park

Prince Albert National Park

Brightsand Lake

Manitou Lake

Redberry Lake

Lake Diefenbaker

South Saskatchewan River

Red Deer River Forks

Great Sand Hills

Cypress Hills

Grasslands National Park

Killdeer Badlands

Selwyn Lake

Hunt Falls and Grease River

Churchill River

Nipekamew Sand Pillars

Steepbank Lake

Gem Lakes

Candle Lake

Rice River

Saskatchewan River Forks

Red Deer River

Kipibiskau Lake

Quill Lakes

Duck Mountain

Good Spirit Lake

Last Mountain Lake

Qu'Appelle River

Avonlea Badlands

Big Muddy Badlands

Souris River

Stony Rapids

La Ronge

Meadow Lake

Prince Albert

Battlefords

Saskatoon

Hudson Bay

Yorkton

Moose Jaw

Regina

Swift Current

Eastend

Estevan

Visitor Resources

Saskatchewan Scenic Secrets is intended as an overview and sampling of the many scenic natural areas throughout Saskatchewan. It is beyond the scope of this book to provide details on visiting these and other locations.

Some of Parkland Publishing's other books do provide how-to information on visiting many Saskatchewan attractions (see next page).

We recommend contacting Tourism Saskatchewan, regional tourism associations, Saskatchewan Provincial Parks, and tourism operators offering excursions. Listed here are some operators who assisted us in obtaining photographs, and who offer quality trips and services.

The vast majority of places portrayed in this book are accessible to the public. However, in a few instances, we have indicated that the photography locations are on private land. It is essential to obtain the permission of land owners before entering private land.

Tourism Saskatchewan
Toll-free phone: 1-877-237-2273
www.sasktourism.com

Saskatchewan Provincial Parks
Toll-free phone: 1-800-205-7070
www.saskparks.net

Athabasca Eco Expeditions and Blackmur's Athabasca Fishing Lodges
Toll-free phone: 1-877-922-0957
www.athabascalake.com

Selwyn Lake Lodge
Toll free phone: 1-800-667-9556 or 306-933-9453
www.adventuredestinations.ca/html/selwyn/

Sawyer Lake Adventures
306-547-4661
www.sawyerlake.com

Churchill River Canoe Outfitters
1-877-511-2726
www.churchillrivercanoe.com

Other books by Robin and Arlene Karpan

Northern Saskatchewan Canoe Country
Join writers and photographers Robin and Arlene Karpan on a visual journey through northern Saskatchewan's most spectacular rivers and lakes. Famous rivers such as the Churchill, Clearwater, Cree, Fond du Lac, and Sturgeon-weir flow through a vast forested land of 100,000 lakes. Follow in the wake of voyageurs with fur-laden birchbark canoes, aboriginal artists who painted mystical images on riverside cliffs, and a who's who of northern exploration. It's all here – a compelling history, jaw-dropping scenery, plenty of adrenaline-pumping whitewater, and tranquility to soothe the soul.
Hard cover, 11 x 8 ½, 128 pages, over 200 colour photos, ISBN 978-0-9809419-0-6, $34.95

Saskatchewan Scenic Drives
Head off the major highways and into Saskatchewan's scenic heartland. Follow secondary highways, grid roads, and backroads to spectacular river valleys, forested lakelands, wild badlands, secret hideaways, and awesome vistas. Drive a third of the way across Saskatchewan entirely in the Qu'Appelle Valley. Take a little-known backroad through the Big Muddy Badlands. See Saskatchewan's biggest tree and the other-worldly "Crooked Trees". Precise directions and maps make it easy to discover these and many more Saskatchewan scenic wonders.
Soft cover, perfect bound, 6 x 9, 240 pages 45 b&w maps, 120 b&w photos ISBN 978-0-9683579-6-5, $24.95

Saskatchewan Trails – A Guide to Nature Walks and Easy Hikes (2nd Edition)
Saskatchewan Trails guides you on over 100 nature trails through the province's diverse landscapes, from prairie grasslands to aspen parkland, boreal forest, shield country, badlands, lakelands, and river valleys.
Soft cover, perfect bound, 5 ½ x 8 ½, 288 pages 69 b&w maps, index, 72 b&w photos ISBN 978-0-9683579-4-1, $19.95

Northern Sandscapes – Exploring Saskatchewan's Athabasca Sand Dunes
The Athabasca Sand Dunes are like nowhere else on Earth – a desert-like environment seemingly misplaced in the northern forest. Follow the Karpans on an exciting canoe journey through this stunning wilderness.
Soft cover, perfect bound, 8 ½ x 11, 128 pages 115 colour photos, index, bibliography ISBN 978-0-9683579-0-3, $29.95

Larger Than Life – Saskatchewan's Big Roadside Monuments
Know where to find the world's largest still for making home brew? How about the world's largest moose, bunnock, or white-tailed deer? Why did a Saskatchewan town build a huge Santa Claus, and others build a big pink pig, a lighthouse, or kangaroo rats? Travel to over 70 communities to marvel at massive monuments, and discover the stories behind who built these intriguing sculptures, and why.
Soft cover, perfect bound, 5 ½ x 8 ½, 176 pages 100 b&w photos, ISBN 978-0-9683579-9-6, $18.95

Saskatchewan Trivia Challenge
Where can you find the largest lake in the world that drains into two different oceans, North America's largest collection of rare 13th to 17th century books, or the goat that served in World War I and has the medals to prove it? They're all in Saskatchewan. *Saskatchewan Trivia Challenge* answers these and over 240 other intriguing questions on Saskatchewan's biggest, best, firsts, records, famous folks, oddities, and just plain "cool stuff".
Soft cover, perfect bound, 5 ½ x 8 ½, 192 pages 85 b&w photos, ISBN 978-0-9683579-2-7, $14.95

Saskatoon History Trivia Quest
Discover Saskatoon's fascinating past – famous and colourful characters, accomplishments, the flamboyant boosterism of the boom years, and tidbits of oddball stuff that contributed to the development of Saskatchewan's largest city.
Soft cover, perfect bound, 5 ½ x 8 ½, 176 pages 100 b&w photos, ISBN 978-0-9683579-8-9, $16.95

Western Canadian Farm Trivia Challenge
It's time to have some fun with farming. Do you know how much a cow pie weighs, how many litres of milk a dairy cow produces each day, or the prairie community that built a bronze statue to honour a pig that escaped from the abattoir? All is revealed in *Western Canadian Farm Trivia Challenge*.
Soft cover, perfect bound, 5 ½ x 8 ½, 192 pages 66 b&w photos, ISBN 978-0-9683579-5-8, $14.95

Available at fine bookstores, or from Parkland Publishing. Phone: 306-242-7731 www.parklandpublishing.com

FINAL FRAME: *Jade Lake, one of the Gem Lakes in Narrow Hills Provincial Park.*